The Santa Muerte Spell Book

Isabella Macias

Copyright © 2022 Isabella Macias
All rights reserved.
Cover Photo: CC BY-ND 2.0 Thomas Altfather Good

CONTENTS

Part I – The Basics 3

Altar Preparation 5

Altar Tools 9

Consecrating Ritual 11

Opening Your Psychic Abilities 13

Spiritual or Ritual Baths 23

Magia Verde: Herbs in Spellwork 27

Part II – the Spell Book of Santa Muerte 35

To Gain Santa Muerte's Assistance 37

Bring Blessings To The Home 40

Attract Prosperity 41

'Limpia' To Attract Luck 42

Using Parsley For Good Luck 43

For Success 44

Obtain Success 45

Finding Employment 46

Using Amenia For Finding Employment 47

For A Business 48

To Uncross A Jinxed Business 49

For Love 50

Using An Image Candle To Conquer A Loved One 51

For Healing 52

To Stop Addictions 53

Child Support/Things Related To Children 54

Against Rumors 55

Psychic Attack..57

For Protection..58

How To Remove The Evil Eye 59

Triangle Of Protection 60

Cleansing Against Envy..61

Remove Enemies...62

Send Back Witchcraft 63

Destroy A Person..64

Part III – Powerful Prayers..65

Avoid Accidents 67

Attract Money...68

Attract Good Friends 69

Break A Hex..70

Bring Peace To Feuding Families 71

Change One's Luck...72

Comfort Those In Trouble..73

Conquer One's Fears 74

Freedom From Guilt 75

For Health 76

Courage To Confront Problems...77

Courage To Face One's Enemies 78

Finding Employment 79

Gain Confidence 80

Guidance/Wisdom 81

Protect One's Home 82

Reunite Lovers 83

Reverse Evil Back To One's Enemies 84

Spiritual Growth 85

Success In One's Endeavors 86

When Justice Has Been Served 87

Amparo Against Witchcraft 91

Santa Muerte Novena 92

Miraculous Muerte Prayer 95

To Repay Santa Muerte for Her Favors 96

¡ADVERTENCIA!

This book is designed to provide information with respect to the subject matters addressed. Nothing contained in any part is to be construed as medical, legal, or other related advice. The information contained herein should always be used in a moral and ethical manner. Any misuse of this information is not condoned by the author or publisher. The reader should and will accept all responsibilities in the study and respect of this subject matter. .

PART I

THE BASICS

ALTAR PREPARATION

The first thing a Bruja/Brujo in training. needs to learn is how to set up an altar. The altar serves as a channel in calling spirits and telling them that you wish to gain their guidance and assistance in the work you are now willing to dedicate yourself to.

The altar should be in a room inside (or outside) your home that no one uses. When you decide which room your altar is going to be in, begin by washing the interior of the room with a good soap mixed with amenia. Next, go outside and take three branches off of a tree; make sure they have leaves. Go inside the room and pour amenia over the branches. Now, walk around the room and hit the walls with the branches simultaneously. Pick up any leaves that have fallen on the with anything but your bare hands. After you have finished, light some pleasant-smelling incense.

If you feel that the cleansing you just did was not powerful enough to rid a negative entity which may still be lingering inside your room do the following: place in a triangular form, in the center of your room, a seven-day candle of St. Alex, St. Martin de Porres. and St. Cipriano. Beside each candle place a glass that is filled half way with water. To the right side of the candles light a couple of incense sticks of saffron. Light the candles and pray an 'Our Father' aloud. Each day for the next six days you will go before the candles and pray the same prayer. Do not extinguish the candles yourself, let them burn out.

It is now time to look for a table to make an altar out of. The size of the table is unimportant. Choose one that you feel comfortable with.

After you have the table which you will be using as an altar, take it outside and scrub it with soap mixed with amenia. When the water dries, paint the table white. Let the paint dry. Once the paint has dried, cut three branches from a tree. Pour amenia over them and beat them against the table until you have covered the entire table. If you are going to use chairs along with your altar, you may prepare them the same way you prepared the table.

Take the table and chairs inside your ritual room and place them facing to the west. Next, burn as an incense, a mixture of saffron, frankincense and myrrh.

Place a white sheet over your altar table. In the center you will place a large beeswax candle and beside it place a clear glass of water. While the candle is burning, pick a time during the day, in which you can you can sit in front of the candle and meditate. Each morning throw the water in the glass over your front porch. Refill the glass with fresh water and place it back on the altar.

Place your statue of Santa Muerte in the center. Creating your altar to the Santa Muerte is like creating an altar on the day of the dead; there are not really any rules about what to put, but I suggest some of the following things:

- A bottle of tequila, mezcal, red wine, beer, rum, brandy, whiskey, cognac or whatever you drink. You will take the bottle and fill two glasses, one you will take and the other you will leave to the saint, do it once a month, she will drink her glass little by little, but do not let it empty, fill it every time it is necessary.
- A pack of cigarettes or cigars, you will still smoke one and light one every month, leave the rest there.
- Flowers, if they are natural, you will change them every time they wither, they can be plastic but do not let them get dirty.
- Water, a glass of water since water purifies the same, don't let her drink it empty, don't let her glass empty.
- Bread since it represents abundance.

- Candles or candles, they represent the light to souls and your life, you can always have one on or light them only when you make requests, but remember not to leave them unattended to avoid an accident, you can light a white candle or candle, but every Color has a meaning, red-love, gold-yellow money, brown work, health-green, protection or work from black damage, clean purple, blue study or exams, orange legal problems.
- Chocolates and apples, which is the sweetness of life and are used for labors of love since they sweeten relationships, the same happens with apples.

From there you can put what you want such as food, drinks, sweets, sugar, honey, toys, dishes, etc. The only rule is that nothing is spoiled, or allowed to get dirty or rot, a neglected altar will not work, remember that everything is symbolism, that is, if you put a plate of chicken with mole, it is the same whether it is real or figurative of ceramic, crumb or other material, if it is real it can only be on the altar for one or two days due to the decomposition process never let flies or cockroaches flow on your altar that will be an offense and far from pleasing will be the opposite.

Opening Prayers
Our Father

Our Father, who art in Heaven, hallowed be thy name. Thy kingdom come, Thy will be done, on earth as it is in heaven. Give us this day our daily bread, and forgive us our trespasses, as we forgive those who trespass against us. And lead us not into temptation, but deliver us from evil. Amen.

Hail Mary (X3)

Hail Mary, full of grace, the Lord is with thee. Blessed art thou among women and blessed is the fruit of thy womb, Jesus. Holy Mary, Mother of God pray for us

sinners, now and at the hour of our death. Amen.
Glory Be
Glory be to the Father, to the Son, and to the Holy Spirit, as it was in the beginning, is now, and ever shall be, world without end. Amen.
St. Michael
St. Michael, the Archangel, defend us in our day of battle. Be our safeguard against the wickedness and snares of the Devil. May God rebuke him, we humbly pray, and do thou, O Prince of the Heavenly Host, by the power of God, thrust into Hell Satan and the other evil spirits who prowl through the world seeking the ruin of souls. Amen.
Invocational Prayer
Almighty God, before your Divine Presence, (sign of the cross) in the name of the Father, Son, and Holy Spirit, we ask permission to invoke Santa Muerte. Holy and Powerful Mother, at this moment we beg for your presence and intervention. Through the great power, which God has given you, we beg of you to hear our prayers and grant us all the favors we ask of you until the last day, hour, and moment when the Divine Majesty shall call us before his presence. Santa Muerte, beloved of my heart, do not abandon me without your protection. *(✠ Sign of the cross)* In the name of the Father, the Son , and the Holy Spirit. Amen.

Ending Prayers
In the name of the Father, the Son, and the Holy Spirit; *(✠ Sign of the cross)* Santa Muerte, Our Most Holy Mother, I beseech you lovingly to protect those who carry your prayers and devoutly honor you. Cover them with your mantle, and guard them with your scythe, that their enemies may not have dominion over them. Protect them from bad luck, disease, and envy; witchcraft, hexes, and curses; lightning, fires, and earthquakes; demons, evil spirits, and phantoms; evil eyes, evil hearts, and evil minds; cover them, oh Holy Mother, so that no evil can see them, no evil can touch them, and no evil can follow them. In

the name of the Father, the Son, and the Holy Spirit. Amen.

Our Father (X3).

ALTAR TOOLS

In order to make your altar complete, you need tools which must accompany your altar.

One of these tools is a glass of water which will serve as an offering to the spirits around you. If you would like to add a pinch of salt to the water, go ahead. Some Brujas and Brujos keep a glass of water as the offering and another glass with salt water to use during meditation. Use which ever method you feel comfortable with.

You may, if you wish, sprinkle pure jasmine oil on your altar since it is a fragrance known to attract helpful and knowledgeable spirits.

Another tool which you will use is a watch or a clock. When you pray to God or his angelic spirits for a special petition, it usually takes a while for it to materialize. Therefore, the ticking of the clock is telling the spirits assisting you to work quickly so that your wish can materialize sooner than it otherwise would.

A tool which is an important part of Brujeria is the dagger. Place the dagger on top of your altar once you have consecrated it. It is used to make magical circles and to tear evil forms of magic directed at you.

On the next page you will be given a consecrating ritual which you can use to purify any objects that will be placed on your altar.

CONSECRATING RITUAL

Consecrating is just a way of cleansing and purifying objects which you will use in your work. The ritual used to consecrate need not be long or complicated.

The following ritual is used to consecrate your altar tools. Keep in mind that this is just an outline to give you an idea as to how the ritual is done. As you grow spiritually, change or lengthen the ritual. Consecrate your altar tools by doing the following:

Burn as an incense a mixture of copal and St. John's wort. Pass the object through the smoke and say "I cleanse and purify thee with air."

Dip the object into a cup which contains a tea made of hyssop. As you do this say the following "With water I cleanse and purify thee."

Light a white candle. Pass the object through the flame without burning your fingers. As you do this say "With fire I burn all impurities and cleanse thee so that you will be in accord with me. "

OPENING YOUR PSYCHIC ABILITIES

All of us are born with different types and degrees of psychic ability or intuition. Some are in tune to them more than others and therefore use it more easily than others. Just like there are people who have a natural ability for mathematics and have no trouble with numbers, others struggle their entire lives with anything beyond the basics. Like everything else a person wants to get good at it takes time, practice, and determination to master these intuitive skills.

Energy

Ever wonder why some people have "it" and others don't. Well the natural ability of some is really best summed up as a pool of energy (sometimes called power). We are all born with some inherent energy. Day to day life drains that energy from the first moments of socialization. It is a life long struggle to rekindle and maintain the energy that most every sentient being has naturally from birth.

A study of most religions and cultures will lead even the most casual observer to the techniques mankind has found to generate energy, maintain and utilize it. Some direct examples can be found in yoga, karate or kung fu. Of course, you can also find examples in the strict ways that monks or holy men live in many religions.

It is not by chance that most religions share commonality in their methods.

So it is important to understand that some effort may not be enough to open your psychic abilities. One must delve into the mystery of energy and power to fully explore this subject. And, a one sure means towards that end can be found in the practice of meditation.

Meditation

Meditation is the most important thing you can do to

open your psychic mind. Given that you have enough psychic energy, meditation helps you to focus on receiving and interpreting messages. It also helps you to connect with spirits there to offer their assistance. Meditation brings you closer to a world we cannot see and brings together the mind, body, and spirit as a whole. Only through meditation can a person achieve complete stillness of the mind and experience deep awareness. This stillness is essential to opening the psychic abilities within you.

Awareness

When developing your psychic abilities, awareness is just as important as meditation. Without a keen sense of awareness, it will be extremely difficult if not impossible to receive and interpret messages given to you.

There are things you can practice to develop your awareness but the operative word here is practice. For instance, when you're out in public instead of only concentrating on what you are doing, try to see how many sounds are taking place around you; how many people you hear talking, how many children are talking or crying. You can also use this method in natural areas such as a park or even in your own backyard. Go outside, sit down and close your eyes. Try to hear all the sounds around you. Listen to all the different noises from nature such as birds, bugs, and the wind. Use your awareness to actually "feel" the warmth of the sun or the coldness of the winter. Try to notice different aromas. When you look at a tree, don't notice the leaves but the space between them. Use all of your senses and even use them in different ways. If you practice building your awareness everyday you will greatly increase your intuition at the same time.

Take Note

When practicing, you might want to get a small notebook to write down your experiences every time you meditate or when you are building your awareness. Here you can keep notes as to feelings you pick up, how your mind or body reacts, or images that enter your mind. Also write down any thoughts that come up and if you find yourself disturbed write down what caused the disturbance. Write down everything you experience even if you don't think it's related to your practices. Many times by keeping notes you'll find patterns that develop which could be of help to you.

The Feeling

Many people have certain things that happen to them which gives them a clue that they are about to receive a message from the spirit world. Some people may get an empty feeling in the pit of their stomach right before they pick up on a message or before they have a vision. Others may get a numbness in their forehead, hands, feet, or any other part of their body. Some have a buzzing in their ears. This is another reason your awareness must be strengthened so that you will be able to understand when these things are happening. The signs can be anything and they can be different from person to person so being aware is a very important tool.

Saint Gabriel

Many people don't realize that St Gabriel, the archangel, helps in psychic ability, intuition, and receptivity.

This is probably because it isn't widely talked about. St Gabriel helps the gifted psychic either to properly use their gift or to strengthen their gift and will also help those who wish to develop and sharpen their intuitive skills. St Gabriel also helps you by making it easier to receive and understand messages. So "adopting" this archangel as one you would honor and pray to everyday will prove to be a very rewarding practice.

You can begin working with St Gabriel by first reading everything there is to read about this angel. You must familiarize yourself with this angel as much as you possibly can. Once you think you have a good understanding of this angles background, how this angel came to be and how this angel works, you can begin working with St Gabriel.

Note: Even though it's thought that a person shouldn't honor the archangels, they do however have dominion over certain areas that are permissible to explore.

If you decide you want to invoke the help of St Gabriel, it would be a good idea to set up an altar in honor of this powerful angel. The altar can be placed just about anywhere in your home that you wish with a few exceptions. The altar should never be placed near a restroom, in the kitchen or in a closet. If there is a

particular place in the home that you will be doing your meditation that room would be an excellent place to set it up.

At the altar is where you can light candles to St Gabriel, leave special offerings such as incense, gemstones, small angel statues, or hand written requests, or anything else you feel St Gabriel will like or can help with.

Many times your intuition will come into play and you will "just know" what to place on the altar. Before you meditate or practice your awareness exercises, go to the altar and offer St Gabriel a white votive candle, and offer a prayer to guide you and to help sharpen your intuition. That's all there is to it. Just make sure you keep the altar clean and free of dust and throw away all used candles. Keep the area neat and clean.

Within a short time you will notice a difference in your concentration, intuition and hunches.

The Wind

Another entity you might be interested in working with is the spirit of the wind. Because it travels everywhere, the wind is therefore part of everything around us, everything that ever was and everything that will ever be. It knows all secrets, all things past, present and future. The spirit of the wind, if invoked and utilized in the proper way can give insight into anything a person wants to know... literally. This spirit is glad to share the knowledge it possesses but devotion, prayer and offerings are expected in return.

Setting up an altar to this entity is important to working with it. The colors in either fabric used or candles burned are important. If you want to use some fabric as an altar cloth, choose either very pale blues, any shade of yellows, or any shade of white. For candles offered to this spirit choose either yellow or white, no blue candles. Offerings can include wind chimes, statues or pictures of birds, especially white doves, any kind of flowers in any color, quartz crystals, and floral scented incense. The altar should be set up in a location where there is a window near, not directly in front of a window but rather off to the side. Keep the altar free from dust and free from dead or dying plants. Once plants begin to wilt throw them away and discard used candles.

Here at this altar you will actually call the entity to come and assist when you are practicing or doing any kind of divination practice. This includes divination in any form whether it's thru mind reading, card reading, or any other method. After calling the spirit, offer a candle in its honor. You can also light some incense if you want, then say a prayer in your own words asking for help in opening your psychic eye or to sharpen your intuition. Whatever you happen to be working towards at the time can be asked.

Once you have made contact with the wind, you will not want to expose yourself unnecessarily to it during the hours of dawn and dusk. We are all most susceptible during these times and can waste valuable energy.

Other Spirits

Besides the helpful spirits that roam the earth who once had human form and passed into the dimension of the spirit, there are also entities who have never been born but who are still very real. They can also be called on for help in developing your intuitive skills. Please keep in mind that they are unlike us in most every aspect and they can act in unforeseen ways. Do not trust just any spirit you encounter. As in life, treachery and deceit are as common as help and assistance when dealing with spirits. Always use extreme caution when communicating with the spirit world.

The Third Eye

I will now give you one more method to developing your psychic abilities. I don't remember how or where I came across this method but when I found it I decided I'd give it a try. To my amazement from the first time I applied this method I began to feel a tingling in between my eyebrows (the third eye). I used this method in its entirety out of curiosity and still to this day I use it to keep the channels open. This is a very powerful method and most often people will actually feel a difference the first time it is used. This method has two stages that one must follow. Each stage is very important and should be followed in turn. Do not begin with the second stage until you have completely gone through the entire first stage.

Stage 1: Awakening the Third Eye

This is done with a specific tone and mantra. You only need to do this exercise for 3 days. Afterwards, it is permanent. The mantra to be used is "Thoh" pronounced "TOE". It must be within the correct tone. Not a deep tone and not a high pitched tone, but rather a tone that is in between the two, like an alto range. You will feel it in between your eyebrows when you hit the correct tone. So when you are chanting this mantra, use different voice levels and when you feel that vibration between your brows you know that's the correct one. Practice the tone first before following the steps below.

1. Sit with your back straight. Sit on the floor if possible.

2. Breathe in through your nose and hold your breath as long as you comfortably can. Then slightly open your jaws so there is a small space between your top and bottom teeth and place the tip of your tongue between the space of your slightly parted teeth.

3. Put a very light pressure on the tongue with your teeth. This is like the same process of saying the "TH" part of the English word "the." Once your tongue is in position, release your breath slowly through your mouth saying T-H-H-O-H-H in one long exhale (say the word one time per exhale). Your tongue will be vibrating between your teeth. You should feel the air moving past your tongue and teeth. If this technique is done properly, you will feel a pressure or sensation in your jaw and cheeks. The tone will also vibrate in your 3rd eye. It may take a few seconds to adjust this, don't worry, just keep going.

4. Do the above 5 times in a row.

5. It is very important that the above exercise be done once per day for 3 consecutive days, 24 hours apart. Then it is a done deal.

What You Can Expect:

1. You may experience a headache or a pressure in the center of the forehead. This sensation may also feel like it is originating from within, usually an inch or more beneath the surface of the forehead. This is a positive indication that the third eye is awakening and beginning to function in a healthy manner.

2. You may also feel a throbbing or tingling sensation in your forehead. This may feel like goose bumps or like your skin is crawling. This feeling may be very intense like something is there.

The sensation of pulsing, throbbing or tingling will continue throughout the day. This is the final
physiological event you will experience after opening up your 3rd eye. It indicates your pineal gland is awakened, functioning and alive.

Psychic Effects:

Faster, easier learning and retention, marked with an increase in intuition ¾ Increased creativity
Psychic gifts developing and becoming remarkably strong and intense
An ability to see human auras
Clairaudience (psychic hearing) begins to open

Please make sure you have fully accomplished the first stage before moving on. If necessary, start again with the beginning of the first stage until you are satisfied that it has worked.

Stage 2: Keeping the Third Eye Open and Functioning

In order for this to work properly, you must have already performed the stage 1 awakening exercise. It is very important to wait for 10-14 days after completing stage 1 before going to stage 2. Otherwise the exercises won't be as effective since your body needs time to adapt and get the energy flow going. Unlike stage 1 which is performed once, this stage should be done at least once a week to maintain and keep the third eye open.

1. Breathe in deeply and hold your breath for a count of 5, 3 times. This helps you to become relaxed and focused. Then focus all of your concentration on your 3rd eye (the spot between your brows). You should start to

feel a sensation similar to the effects of the first stage exercise like a slight pressure or awareness of the spot of your 3rd eye.

2. Now, take a deep breath as you did for the awakening one exercise. Hold it for as long as you comfortably can and release your breath vibrating the word "MAY." Pronounced like the English word for the month of May. It should all come out at one time- M-a-a-a-a-a-a-a-a-a-y.

Gradually and slowly. It is ok to adjust your pitch again.

3. Breathe in again. Repeat step 2, 5 times in total. The tone should be alto. You need to hit a certain pitch. You will know, for you will feel this in your head. Do the best you can.

Now, this is very important...when vibrating the word "MAY," feel the energy going into your head, first your 3rd eye area, then into the middle of your brain and then to the top of your head where your crown chakra is located (the soft spot of a baby's head). Remember to concentrate on your forehead (3rd eye area), then the middle of your brain and finally the top of your head. This is done for the duration of each chant.

Here are the steps simplified:
1. Breathe in
2. Begin to exhale, vibrating "MAY"
3. Concentrate on your 3rd eye
4. Concentrate on the middle of your brain
5. Concentrate on the top of your head and finish exhaling the vibration

Repeat 4 more times.

The effects of this exercise are extremely pleasurable. A feeling of lightness can occur immediately following. Some people may feel energy or tingling inside their heads, or completely covering their heads; a slight pressure in the crown area and intense euphoria. The bliss state can occur for hours and even days later. This will become permanent and will greatly assist in meditation, clairvoyance and other psychic and paranormal powers. Practice and you will find an expanded range of your intuitive and psychic abilities.

Building your energy through meditation and the assistance of guides is often critical in having success. Always use common sense when exploring the spirit world as you never want to invite something unknown into your place. Remember that there are spirits that would like to meet you as much as you would like to meet them... but for different reasons. This is not a game. The consequences from not ensuring your own protection or irresponsible actions can be devastating. You have been warned.

SPIRITUAL OR RITUAL BATHS

Many cultures believe in the powerful effects of water not only for cleaning the mundane dirt from our bodies but to cleanse our spirit, our soul and our essence. Spiritual bathing, also known as ritual bathing, is as old as mankind and is still practiced today.

Spiritually Cleansing Energy
Spiritual baths are related to healing practices throughout the world. These baths strengthen our connection with nature and brings us closer to God. They can be taken for inner guidance and to uplift the soul even for those who do not hold any particular religious or spiritual beliefs. Depending on the spiritual bath taken these baths can help end bad luck, open the way for love, happiness, money, healing, and just about any situation a person may face.

Spiritual Cleansing removes all the negative energy from your body and aura that is collected from day to day. Your body acts like a sponge that collects the energies that you come in contact with on a daily basis.

This accumulation of energies is not released on its own. Instead it is collected over a period of time and becomes mixed, stagnant and stale. Often it creates blocks and obstacles. Some of these energies are good while other energies are negative. Just like the air we breathe… It cannot be seen, but we know it is there.

We live off of it. We feel it on our skin. The same is true about the energies we collect. These energies are not visible, but still have profound effects on every aspect of our lives.

The Bath Ritual

There is a certain procedure that needs to be followed

when taking these types of baths.

When you are trying to "bring" or "attract" something stand in the tub and pour the water over your head and then rub your body upwards with your hands from your feet to your head. The idea here is that you want to rub the spiritual water that you poured over yourself back up the body to "bring" results.

When you are trying to send something "away", "repel" or "rid" yourself of something then you want to pour the water over your head and then rub your body downwards with your hands from your head to your feet.

The idea here is that you want to rub the spiritual water that you poured over yourself down the body to "rid" a problem.

Whichever result you are seeking you should first shower beforehand to remove the mundane dirt from the body, turn off the shower or empty the tub and then stand there and pour the spiritual water over yourself.

Once you pour the spiritual water over yourself, do not dry off. Allow the moisture to dry naturally.

The Moon

If you really want to add some extra power to these baths look at the moon cycle.

When applying the moon phases in your spiritual baths the rule is to take your spiritual bath during the waning moon when you want to "remove" or "repel" something and if you want to "draw" or "attract" something then take your spiritual bath during the waxing moon.

There are numerous places on the net that give the current phase of the moon. There are also moon phase programs you can download for free that will tell you what phase the moon is currently in and when a particular moon phase will happen… do some research…it is easy to find.

Bath Mixtures

Here are some bath mixtures you can try for yourself:

Note: When I mention a handful as a measurement this does not mean as much as your hand will hold. Use only enough herb to make a small bundle to cover your palm.

Emotional Bath

This is a good bath if you have fears, phobias, nightmares, depression or anxiety.

1 handful rue
1 handful basil
1 handful sage

Boil 1 quart of filtered water and remove from heat. Place the herbs in the water and allow to steep until the water is cool to the touch. Strain out the herb and use the liquid for the bath.

Energy Clearing Bath

This is a good bath to remove any negative energy you have collected.

1 handful of sea salt
1 handful of either rosemary or sage (rosemary is good for your hair and scalp too)

Boil 1 quart of filtered water and remove from heat. Place the herbs in the water and allow to steep until the water is cool to the touch. Strain out the herb and use the liquid for the bath.

Saint Michael Bath

This is a good bath for spiritual protection.

1 handful angelica

Boil 1 quart of filtered water and remove from heat. Place the herbs in the water and allow to steep until the water is cool to the touch. Strain out the herb and use the liquid for the bath.

San Martin Caballero Bath

This is a good bath for success.

1 handful of honeysuckle
1 handful of mint
2 star anise

Boil 1 quart of filtered water and remove from heat. Place the herbs in the water and allow to steep until the water is cool to the touch. Strain out the herb and use the liquid for the bath.

Healing Bath

2 parts Eucalyptus
1 part Sandalwood

Boil 1 quart of filtered water and remove from heat. Place the herbs in the water and allow to steep until the water is cool to the touch. Strain out the herb and use the liquid for the bath.

La Virgencita De Guadalupe (Virgin of Guadalupe Bath)

This is good bath for love and good luck.

The petals from 7 roses

Boil 1 quart of filtered water and remove from heat. Place the flower petals in the water and allow to steep until the water is cool to the touch. Strain out the herb and use the liquid for the bath. After the bath spray your body with holy water.

MAGIA VERDE: HERBS IN SPELLWORK

This is a short list of some well-known herbs that can be used in Spellwork. Although some of the herbs mentioned can be taken internally, I do not endorse this use here. Please use caution in applying any herbal Spellwork as the results can be dramatic.

Some common uses of herbs in Spellwork are:

To bring the herbs influence into your home, you can plant them in pots as houseplants or grow them in your yard.

To use as a candle dressing, dried and crushed herbs are needed. For candle dressings apply your chosen oil first and sprinkle the chosen herb over the oil so it will stick to the candle.

To bring the herbs influence to you such as luck and prosperity, carry the herb in your pocket.

Angelica
Use: Protection, visions, healing, exorcism, breaks witchcraft, stops evil forces

Alfalfa
Use: To keep a friendship, anti-poverty, luck when asking for loans, prosperity, money

All Heal
Use: Illnesses

African Ginger
Use: Stops curses and hexes

Althaea
Use: Healing, stops nightmares, eases sorrow, attracts good spirits, visions, protection, psychic power, marriage

Aloe
Use: Protection from evil, luck, protection from household accidents, new love

Anise Seed

Use: Protection from evil eye, psychic visions, purification, wards off evil, stops nightmare, strengthen psychic abilities, meditation, astral travel, prophetic dreams
Anise, Star
Use: Lost love, good luck, visions, psychic powers, lust, negative energy, removes obstacles, peace, protection, purification
Asafoetida
Use: Exorcism, purification, break bad habits, health/healing, protection from witchcraft, keeps the law away
Allspice
Use: Good luck, prosperity, business success, money, love
Acacia
Use: Personal power, spirit communication, protection, psychic powers
Agrimony
Use: Protection, sleep, psychic attack, breaks witchcraft
Amaranth
Use: Healing, protection, mends a broken heart
Arbutus
Use: Exorcism, protection
Arrow Root
Use: Good fortune, opportunity, gambling luck
Adam & Eve root
Use: Love, fidelity, lust, happiness
Bayberry
Use: Good luck, money, peace, harmony, prosperity, collecting money owed
Blessed Thistle
Use: Protection, purification, breaks witchcraft, fertility, strengthens family relations
Boneset
Use: To protect from and cure spiritual illness, removes evil energies, breaks witchcraft, exorcism
Basil
Use: Happy homes, money, success, wealth, exorcism,

love, protection, calms anger, courage, peace, prosperity, breaks witchcraft, purifying, luck

Bay Leaves
Use: Purification, psychic power, strength, prophetic dreams, love, romance, protection from witchcraft, money, increase intuition, job promotion, employment, wisdom

Bay Laurel
Use: Protection from negativity and evil

Bergamot
Use: Wealth, money, breaks witchcraft, success, peace, happiness, restful sleep, make good decisions, protection, prosperity, prophetic dreams, attracts good spirits

Bistort
Use: Psychic power, fertility, divination, good fortune, success, money

Borage
Use: Courage, psychic power, family happiness, money, business success

Burdock
Use: Protection, healing, purification

Balm of Gilead
Use: Protection, healing/health, love, relationship problems, encourages reconciliation, gambling luck, fidelity, protect from the evil eye

Buckthorn
Use: Protection, exorcism, legal matters

Buchu
Use: Psychic power, prophetic dreams, divination

Comfrey
Use: Money, safe travel, healing, gambling luck

Cohosh, Black
Use: Love, courage, protection, breaks witchcraft, exorcism, strength, lust, money

Cohosh, Blue
Use: Protection from enemies and evil spirits

Coltsfoot
Use: Love, peace, psychic abilities

Calendula
Use: Court and legal matters, gambling luck
Cleavers
Use: Love, friendship, good communication, protection, remove obstacles
Cascara Sagrada
Use: Legal matters and court cases, money, protection, good luck, astral travel
Cloves
Use: Protection, love, money, attracts the opposite sex, stop gossip, good luck, friendship, prosperity, remove negative energies
Catnip
Use: Love, happiness, attracts good spirits, luck, harmony
Cinnamon
Use: Spirituality, success, lust, love, divination, money, good luck, prosperity, strengthens the bond between people
Chicory
Use: Remove obstacles, gain favors, remove negativity, bring opportunities
Coriander
Use: Love, health/healing, lust, protection, fidelity, peace, longevity, strengthen an existing love relationship
Cinquefoil
Use: Love, money, health, power, wisdom, protection
Cowslip
Use: Healing, youth, treasure finding, unwelcome visitors
Dill
Use: Court matters, breaks love spells, protection, money, make others agree with you
Damiana
Use: Lust, visions, new love, lost love, passion
Dittany of Crete
Use: Attracts the opposite sex, visions, strengthen psychic abilities
Datura

Use: Breaks witchcraft, protection, sleep
Eucalyptus
Use: Breaks witchcraft, repels enemies, personal purification after contact with evil, stop nightmares
Eyebright
Use: Mental power, psychic power, strength, divination, memory, to see the truth, meditation, visions
Elecampane
Use: Love, protection, psychic power, stop anger, peace, meditation
Flax Seed
Use: Protection, visions, beauty, psychic powers, healing, money, divination
Feverfew
Use: Protection from accidents, love, attraction, health/healing
Fennel
Use: Healing, purification, protection from witchcraft, to see the truth, change, to keep the law away, courage, longevity
Frankincense
Use: Protection, exorcism, spirituality, cleansing, love, meditation, clairvoyance, justice, strength
Fenugreek
Use: Money, prosperity, promotions/raises, luck, wealth, success
Galangal
Use: Breaks witchcraft, psychic powers, health, money, protection, legal matters, court cases, success, courage, strength, lust, reverse/return work, change
Garlic
Use: Protection, healing, exorcism, lust, anti-theft, cleansing, courage, attraction, love, money, stop gossip/slander
Ginger
Use: Love, money, success, power, passion, good luck, courage

Ginseng
Use: Love, wishes, protection, luck, spirit communication, visions, divination, male vigor, gambling luck, to control another

Hyssop
Use: Cleansing, breaks witchcraft, purification, protection, psychic abilities, protection from theft, protection from the evil eye

Heliotrope
Use: Exorcism, prophetic dreams, wealth, money, power, luck, protection, psychic abilities, finding lost objects

Holy Thistle
Use: Purification, breaks witchcraft

Juniper
Use: Male virility, love, protection from theft, exorcism, passion, good fortune, money

Lemon Verbena
Use: Purification, love, luck, protection, cleansing, peaceful home, to save a bad marriage

Lemongrass
Use: Lust, psychic power, protection, health/healing, attraction, meditation, trance states

Lemon Balm
Use: Success, love, attracts opposite sex, remove evil spirits, fertility

Lavender
Use: Passion, romance, harmony, friendship, longevity, cooperation, relationship problems, spirit communication, happy home

Mugwort
Use: Safe travel, strength, astral travel, prophetic dreams, divination, visions

Marjoram
Use: Protection from witchcraft, money, happiness, love, friendship, divination

Mistletoe
Use: Protection against misfortune of every kind, love

drawing, fertility, friendship, opens locks
Mint
Use: Money, love, lust, mental strength, jealousy/envy, attracts good spirits, prosperity, psychic abilities
Marigold
Use: Protection, prophetic dreams, legal matters, psychic power, visions, find stolen property, gossip, money, psychic abilities, love, to know who stole from you, to know if a partner has cheated
Nutmeg
Use: Gambler's luck, money
Nettle
Use: Exorcism, protection, breaks witchcraft, wards off evil, purification, courage
Poppy Seeds
Use: Domination, to weaken enemies, to cause confusion
Pennyroyal
Use: Keep peace in home, end family troubles, strength, protection, peace, remove obstacles, breaks witchcraft
Rosemary
Use: Gives women dominion in home, fidelity, protection, love, mental power, protection, exorcism, cleansing, longevity, prosperity, prophetic dream, stop nightmares, wisdom
Rue
Use: Healing/health, mental powers, exorcism, love, breaks witchcraft, protection, cleansing, purification, business success, attracts customers, brings opportunities
Sage
Use: Reverse spells, wisdom, longevity, wisdom, protection, wishes, money, remove obstacles, cleansing, purification, health/healing
St. John's Wort
Use: Health, power, protection, strength, love, happiness, confidence, to control a person/situation
Vervain
Use: Love, purification, peace, money, youth, chastity,

healing, protection, cleansing, wealth, stop nightmares, passion, good luck

Wormwood

Use: Calling spirits, protection, love, psychic power, visions, spirit communication, success, prophetic dreams

Yarrow

Use: Breaks witchcraft, psychic power, love, exorcism, courage, marriage, friendship

PART II

THE SPELL BOOK
OF
SANTA MUERTE

TO GAIN SANTA MUERTE'S ASSISTANCE

9 White Taper Candles
Santa Muerte Oil
Copal

Starting on a Friday, each night for nine nights you will offer a glass of water, light a white taper candle anointed with Santa Muerte oil and burn copal in her honor. Then pray:

Opening Prayers
Our Father

Our Father, who art in Heaven, hallowed be thy name. Thy kingdom come, Thy will be done, on earth as it is in heaven. Give us this day our daily bread, and forgive us our trespasses, as we forgive those who trespass against us. And lead us not into temptation, but deliver us from evil. Amen.

Hail Mary (X3)

Hail Mary, full of grace, the Lord is with thee. Blessed art thou among women and blessed is the fruit of thy womb, Jesus. Holy Mary, Mother of God pray for us sinners, now and at the hour of our death. Amen.

Glory Be

Glory be to the Father, to the Son, and to the Holy Spirit, as it was in the beginning, is now, and ever shall be, world without end. Amen.

St. Michael

St. Michael, the Archangel, defend us in our day of battle. Be our safeguard against the wickedness and snares of the Devil. May God rebuke him, we humbly pray, and do thou, O Prince of the Heavenly Host, by the power of God, thrust into Hell Satan and the other evil spirits who prowl through the world seeking the ruin of souls. Amen.

Invocational Prayer

Almighty God, before your Divine Presence, (sign of the cross) in the name of the Father, Son, and Holy Spirit, we ask permission to invoke Santa Muerte. Holy and Powerful Mother, at this moment we beg for your presence and intervention. Through the great power, which God has given you, we beg of you to hear our prayers and grant us all the favors we ask of you until the last day, hour, and moment when the Divine Majesty shall call us before his presence. Santa Muerte, beloved of my heart, do not abandon me without your protection. *(✠ Sign of the cross)* In the name of the Father, the Son, and the Holy Spirit. Amen.

Then pray:

"Santa Muerte, grant me your protection and liberate me from any danger. I ask in the name of Jesus Christ that you bless this water which I place before you. Empower it with wisdom and knowledge, provide for sleep, and my memory. Amen."

Ending Prayers

In the name of the Father, the Son, and the Holy Spirit; *(✠ Sign of the cross)* Santa Muerte, Our Most Holy Mother, I beseech you lovingly to protect those who carry your prayers and devoutly honor you. Cover them with your mantle, and guard them with your scythe, that their enemies may not have dominion over them. Protect them from bad luck, disease, and envy; witchcraft, hexes, and curses; lightning, fires, and earthquakes; demons, evil spirits, and phantoms; evil eyes, evil hearts, and evil minds; cover them, oh Holy Mother, so that no evil can see them, no evil can touch them, and no evil can follow them. In the name of the Father, the Son, and the Holy Spirit. Amen.

Our Father (X3)

In the morning, the petitioner takes three sips from the glass of water in honor of the Trinity, and pours out the rest of the water at their front steps. He or she refills the glass with fresh water each night.

After the 9th night, you may call upon this powerful saint to aid you in your spells by offering an anointed candle to her, knocking nine times upon your altar with your right hand and praying the Opening Prayers and the Invocational Prayer before starting your spell work. All spells in this book can be performed with her powerful intercession. Offer her a glass of water, an anointed candle and copal each Saturday night.

Most botanicas sell "Santa Muerte Oil" for anointing candles. Some practitioners blend their own "Santa Muerte Oil" mixing cinnamon and rue powder, with a few drops of myrrh oil into a base oil, such as castor oil or olive oil.

BRING BLESSINGS TO THE HOME

3 red carnations
3 white carnations
one branch of rosemary

Place the flowers into a vase with water. When the carnations begin to dry up, throw them away and replace them. Do this often to have a more relaxed atmosphere in your home.

ATTRACT PROSPERITY

21 laurel leaves
1 oz .. of vervain
21 drops of geranium oil
3 gallons of water

Boil the vervain and the laurel leaves. As the water begins to boil, pour in the drops of the oil.
At midnight, beneath the light of the full moon, soak your feet in the brew which you have made.

'LIMPIA' TO ATTRACT LUCK

1 oz. of basil
1 oz. of rue
1 oz. of rosemary
21 drops of siete machos oil

Place the herbs into a piece of paper large enough to place all the herbs. Once you have placed the herbs on the paper, pour the oil on them. Fold the paper so that the contents may not spill out. Place the paper beneath your mattress. Throw away the charm after three days. This ritual is done to remove negative vibrations from your aura which are preventing you from enjoying a blissful life.

USING PARSLEY FOR GOOD LUCK

3 oz. of parsley

Place powdered parsley in a jar filled with water. Place the jar behind the front door. If you prefer, you can make a tea out of parsley and pour it into a jar once it cools down. This ritual is said to be infallible in removing bad vibrations from the home and in doing this, it strengthens the auras of the people living there, thus causing them to be luckier and healthier.

Each month as you replace the jar, you may burn some parsley as incense to strengthens the home's aura.

FOR SUCCESS

Santa Muerte seven day glass candle
John the Conqueror incense
John the Conqueror root
Silverweed
Orange flannel bag
Success oil
Two lodestones

Place the herbs and lodestones in the bag. Light the incense and pass the bag through the smoke and say, "With air I consecrate thee."
Light the candle pass the bag through the flame (without setting it on fire) and say, "With fire I consecrate thee to bring my desires unto me"
Open the oil, place your palms above the container and see yourself being the successful person you wish to become. Sprinkle some oil on the bag then say, "With oil I consecrate thee so that an attraction for success you'll be."
Place the bag in front of the candle. While visualizing yourself being successful, chant:

Santa Muerte for me do light the way
So that each tomorrow can be a successful day.

OBTAIN SUCCESS

3 red carnations
Tulip incense
One teaspoon of sugar

Place the carnations into a vase which contains a mixture of sugar and water. For the next seven days, burn the incense and say:

With these flowers and water sweet
Successful I will always be.

FINDING EMPLOYMENT

Sugar (A handful)
1 oz. of basil
1 oz. of rue
3 red carnations
A gallon of water

Make a tea out of the herbs and let it cool. After you have taken a bath, pour the tea over your body and say:

Holy Santa Muerte Give me the strength to support my family, help me find a job where my work is appreciated, guide my steps to the place where they are waiting, engages my mind and my efforts in every action you take, you who you work without rest, that you spend nights in sail, let me find a job where my efforts are well remunerated. I ask you lady, understand my pleas and the sincerity of my request, take me for good way, make me useful wherever I am present, that the doors open and I grant the confidence of a job, for the strength of your magical figure, that my abilities be recognized, send me the grace of a good job! Amen!

For best results begin the ritual on a Friday.

USING AMENIA FOR FINDING EMPLOYMENT

Amenia
A match
A white stick candle

On a Tuesday, form a cross on the floor made of amenia. Light the candle then jump in the form of a cross over the cross you made with amenia while repeating seven times:

I have to find the key
to the job that I have lost.

FOR A BUSINESS

To help a business grow and expand or if you just want to attract customers, do the following:
In your business, you will burn a candle of St Jude, Jesus Malverde and Santa Muerte. Place the candles in a triangular form then light them.
You will burn each day before opening, an incense mixture of cinnamon and nutmeg.
You will make a tea of yellow dock and squill root. Once the tea has cooled, mop the floors and throw the remaining water in front of the store.
Above your doorway place a small green bag with two lodestones, five-finger grass and one buckeye.

TO UNCROSS A JINXED BUSINESS

Double Action candle green/black
Seven day candle of Santa Muerte
Santa Muerte incense

Begin by lighting the double action candle. Burn the black half first then burn the green half.
When you have burnt both sides of the candle, light the the Santa Muerte candle and keep it burning every day that your business is open. It would be a good idea to keep the candle burning at night since that is the time people go out and throw things in front of businesses. Each evening before closing, burn the incense inside your business.

FOR LOVE

3 teaspoons of myrrh
3 teaspoons of rue
A tablespoon of frankincense

Place the herbs on a hot piece of charcoal and let the smoke fill the room.
Next, place the incense on the floor and jump over it in the form of a cross three times. After the third jump, stand in front of the incense and say:

__Santa Muerte, don't let me live alone and away from true love. I ask of you, with all my faith, heart and soul to bring me .•••• (name of loved one) so that he/she can be my husband or wife for the rest of my life, amen.__

If the person you are asking the saint to attract to you, is not for you, she will attract to you someone better.

USING AN IMAGE CANDLE TO CONQUER A LOVED ONE

One red image candle (use a male image for a man and a female image for a woman)
3 tablespoons of sugar
Bewitching oil

Write the person's name on the chest of the image. Rub the oil on the candle while thinking of the person you love Sprinkle sugar over the candle then light it. While thinking of your loved one, repeat the following:

Spirit, body and soul of (person's name)
in behalf of this candle, I want you to
come to me determined and with an open heart.
I ask of you, I dominate· you.
I shall bring you and you shall think of no other but me.

For best results, begin this ritual on a Friday.

FOR HEALING

7 day glass candle of Virgen Guadalupe
7 day glass candle of Pedrito Jaramillo
7 day glass candle of Santa Muerte
Allspice incense
A tea made of rue and basil

Place the candles in the form of a triangle. Light the incense in the room in which the person ill is resting.
If this is not possible, place the incense in front of a picture of the person. Sprinkle the tea around the bed of the person daily. If this too is impossible, sprinkle the tea lightly over the picture.
Each evening before going to bed, visualize the person ill recuperating to full health then pray psalm 24.

TO STOP ADDICTIONS

One Santa Muerte candle
One small glass filled with brandy
Six pictures of the person addicted

Place the pictures in the brandy and let them soak for four hours. Take out one picture out of the glass then light the candle. Once you have lit the candle has been lit, pray seven **'Our Fathers.'** Take the picture and burn it using the flame of the candle. Place the ashes in front of the candle, then say the prayer that is printed on the reverse side of the candle. Repeat the prayer nine times and promise the saint that if she heals you of your addiction that you will in turn, light a candle in her name. After you have finished praying say:

Ashes to ashes, dust to dust
My old life has ended, my new life has begun.

Continue doing the ritual until the candle burns out.

CHILD SUPPORT/THINGS RELATED TO CHILDREN

Santa Muerte candle
Helping Hand incense
Picture of the child

Light the incense. Sit in front of the container in which the incense is burning. Visualize the child being surrounded by a white light. Concentrate for a few minutes. Place the picture beneath the candle. Light the candle and pray psalm 93 nine times. Each day repeat the same process: light the incense and concentrate on the child, pray psalm 93 nine times.

AGAINST RUMORS

One large lock
Seven white stick candles
A small stamp of Santa Muerte
Seven drops of rose water

Dress (anoint) the candle with rose water, then place it near the lock. Light the candle and say the prayer that is on the reverse side of the stamp seven times. After you have said the prayer, say the following (while visualizing the person that is spreading rumors):

You see the way this lock is shut and cannot open
This is the way I want Santa Muerte to shut the mouths of those that speak ill of me

PSYCHIC ATTACK

Psychic attack is the art of using magic on another person without their permission. When black magic is used to harm a person directly, the psychic attack will pierce into the victim's aura (only if the victim is not protected psychically) and cause them to go through emotional breakdowns and unexplainable illnesses.

Sometimes the person doing harm will make himself/herself known to his/her victims. They will go to the person's home and sprinkle powder on the doorsteps or rub fowl smelling oils on the door knobs.

If you feel that someone is doing you harm, don't just stand there and let them ruin your life. Reverse their rnagick and give them a taste of their own medicine.

FOR PROTECTION

If you would like to use candles to protect you and your loved ones from evil influences, do so, by all means. The more comfortable you feel with a ritual the better the results will be. Candles are very good psychic protections because as the flame burns, so does the evil that surrounds you. That is why some seven-day candles leave a black film inside the glass. Sometimes while a candle is burning and it breaks, it usually means that the forces that are around you, overpowered the candle. You can prevent this from happening simply by praying constantly in front of the candle. This process will give added power to the candle so that it can overpower the forces which threaten you.

Items Needed
Santa Muerte seven day candle
Holy water
Copal
Rue

On a lit charcoal burn the copal and rue as an incense in the home every Tuesday and Saturday. Rub holy water on the candle before lighting it. Pray an ***'Our Father'*** then light the candle. This candle is very powerful so use it often.

HOW TO REMOVE THE EVIL EYE

Have you ever gone to a beauty parlor, church or any social gathering where there is always a person in the crowd that keeps staring at you from head to toe? After you left the gathering you felt as if someone was hitting you on the head with a hammer or did your best friend suddenly turn on you? If so, the person that kept staring at you surely put the evil eye on you. The evil eye muddies a person's aura so bad that a person's own family and friends tend to turn on him/her. To remove the evil eye, do the following:

Ingredients:
Alum rock
Egg
Hyssop

Begin by lightly rubbing the egg and alum rock over your body. Start at your head then move down to your feet. Do this for three days then throw both away. After you have thrown the egg and alum rock make a tea of hyssop and pour it on your body after you have taken a bath.

TRIANGLE OF PROTECTION

Three handfuls of white flour
Thirty-six white stick candles
Three glasses of water
A picture of the person seeking protection
A seven-day candle- of the San Cipriano
Three red carnations

With the flour form an unbroken triangle. On top of the triangle place a glass of water and a carnation beside it. On the lower right point of the triangle place the other glass of water and two carnations beside it. On the remaining point place the photo. Beside each point of the triangle, place three candles. Light them and repeat:

> ***Holy spirit come brighten the hearts***
> ***around me so they can do us good.***
> ***Spirit of God, dominate my enemies.***
> ***Fill their hearts with humility and love.***

All stick candles should burn out by themselves. Repeat the ritual for the next three days. At the end of last ritual light, the seven-day candle and let it burn out also.

CLEANSING AGAINST ENVY

One fresh lemon
A purple onion
Jinx Removing oil

Place the lemon and onion inside a small bag. Each day before retiring, get the bag and rub it over your body. Begin at your head and work your way down to your feet. Repeat the cleansing every day for one week then throw the items used into moving water. After you have thrown the items used, anoint yourself with the oil until you feel that your aura has been completely cleansed of negative things sent to you.

REMOVE ENEMIES

One black marker
One large nail
Fresh soil
A hammer

Write on the nail, with the marker, the name of the person that is doing you harm.

Fill a small basket with the soil and then hit the nail with the hammer, as far down as possible.

Next., say:

(Enemy's name) you have to leave me alone, never again will you cross my path.

This ritual should be started when the moon is waning (from the time the moon is full to the time the moon is new).

SEND BACK WITCHCRAFT

A glass jar (size is unimportant)
Old rusted nails would be preferable. If you cannot find any, new nails will suffice.
Broken pieces of glass
A lime
Rue
A fresh piece of aloe
Dill seed
Cumin seed
Amenia

Begin by inserting the broken pieces of glass and the nails. You will now cut a small hole in the lime and insert a paper that has your address and the names of those that you wish to protect, into the lime. Place the lime into the jar. Next, sprinkle the herbs into the jar - sprinkle as much of each herb as you feel comfortable with. Pour in the amenia. After you have poured in the amenia, put the top back on the jar and seal it tightly so the contents will not spill out. Once completed, bury the jar in front of your home. Bury it in a place where you can step on it every day.

DESTROY A PERSON

One tablespoon of amenia
One tablespoon of vinegar
Urine of the person doing the ritual
cup of graveyard dust
A small glass jar

Mix all the ingredients together.
For three days place the jar outside so that it may catch the last rays of the sun. On the fourth day, spill the solution around the enemy's home. If you cannot walk around the entire house, spill the solution on the front porch. Do this on a Saturday.

PART III

POWERFUL PRAYERS

POWERFUL PRAYER TREATMENTS

The rituals that follow consist of two things: faith and prayer. They are done with the use of a seven-day glass candle. These rituals are as effective as the other spells that you have seen in the previous pages. Before lighting the candle, rub it with olive oil unless otherwise stated.

After you have dressed the candle (anointed with oil), you may sprinkle the herb recommended on the candle. You must always remember to place the candles somewhere in your home, preferably on top of your altar, or any place that is away from flammable objects.

Pray the prayer as many times as you like. Believe that you will receive what you ask for; don't be doubtful. Candles turning black and/or breaking are indications that someone is working against you. Keep lighting the candles until they no longer turn black or shatter.

If you do not want to sprinkle the herb on the candle, you may burn it as an incense.

AVOID ACCIDENTS

White candle
Olive oil
Comfrey

Psalm 64 verses 1-5 and 10

"Hear my voice, O God, in my prayer. Preserve my life from fear of the enemy. Hide me from the secret counsel of the wicked; from the insurrection of the workers of iniquity who whet their tongue like a sword and bend their bows to shoot arrows, even bitter words that they may shoot in secret at the perfect; suddenly do they shoot at him and fear not. They encourage themselves in an evil manner; they commune of laying snares privily; they say who shall see them. The righteous shall be glad in the lord and trust in him. The upright in heart shall glory."

ATTRACT MONEY

Money House Blessing candle
Olive oil
Cinnamon

Psalm 72 verses 2-9

" He shall judge thy people with righteousness and the poor with judgement. The mountains shall bring peace to the people and -the little hills by righteousness. He shall judge the poor of the people; he shall save the children of the needy and shall break in pieces the oppressor. They shall fear thee as long as the sun and moon endure throughout all generations. He shall come down like rain upon the mown grass as the showers water the earth. In his days shall the righteous flourish and abundance of peace so long as the moon endureth. He shall have dominion from sea to sea and from the river to the ends of the earth. They that dwell in the wilderness shall bow before him and his enemies shall lick the dust."

ATTRACT GOOD FRIENDS

Orange candle
Olive oil
Hyacinth

Psalm 67

" God be merciful unto us and bless us and cause his face to shine upon us; Selah. That thy way may be known upon earth, thy saving health among all nations. Let the people praise thee, 0 God; let all the people thee. 0 let the nations be glad and sing for joy; for thou shalt judge the people righteously and govern the nations upon earth; Selah. Let the people praise thee, O God; let all the people praise thee. Then shall the earth yield her increase and God shall bless us. God shall bless us and all the ends of the earth shall fear him."

BREAK A HEX

White Sanata Muerte Candle
Olive oil
Dill seed

Psalm 25 verses 13-17

" His soul shall dwell at ease and his seed shall inherit the earth. The secret of the lord is with them that fear him; he will show them his covenant. Mine eyes are ever toward the Lord for he shall pluck my feet out of the net. Turn unto me and have mercy upon me for I am desolate and afflicted. The troubles of my heart are enlarged. O God, Bring thou me out of my distresses."

BRING PEACE TO FEUDING FAMILIES

White Santa Muerte candle
Olive oil
Rose petals

Psalm 100

" Make a joyful noise unto the Lord all ye lands. Serve the Lord with gladness; come before his presence with singing. Know ye that the Lord, he is God; it is he that has made us, and not we ourselves. We are his people and the sheep of his pasture. Enter into his gates with thanksgiving and into his courts with praise; be thankful unto him and bless his name. For the Lord is good; his mercy is everlasting and his truth endureth to all generations."

CHANGE ONE'S LUCK

Rainbow Santa Muerte candle
Olive oil
Honeysuckle

Psalm 20

" The Lord hear thee in the day of trouble; the name of the God of Jacob defend thee. Send thee help from the sanctuary and strengthen thee out of Zion. Remember all thy offerings and accept thy burnt sacrifice; Selah. Grant thee according to thine own heart and fulfil all thy counsel. We will rejoice in thy salvation and in the name of our God we will set up our banners; the Lord fulfil all thy petitions. Now know I that the Lord saveth his anointed; he will hear him from his holy heaven with the saving strength of his right hand. Some trust in chariots and some in horses but we will remember the name of the Lord our God. They are brought down and fallen but we are risen and stand upright. Save, Lord: let the king hear us when we call."

COMFORT THOSE IN TROUBLE

White Santa Muerte candle
Olive oil
Jasmine

Psalm 62 verses 5-8

" My soul wait thou only upon God for my expectation is from him. He only is my rock and my salvation; he is my defense; I shall not be moved. In God is my salvation and my glory. The rock of my strength and my refuge, is in God. Trust in him at all times ye people. Pour out your heart before him. God is a refuge for us. Selah."

CONQUER ONE'S FEARS

Santa Muerte candle
Olive oil
Vervain

Psalm 57 verses 2 and 3

" I will cry unto God, be merciful unto me for my soul trusteth in thee; yea, in the shadow of thy wings will I make my refuge until these calamities be overpast. I will cry unto God most high: unto God that performeth all things for me."

FREEDOM FROM GUILT

Lemon Verbena
White candle
Olive oil

Psalm 145 verses 17-21

"The lord is righteous in all his ways and holy in all his works. The lord is nigh unto all them that call upon him; to all that call upon him in truth. He will fulfill the desire of them that fear him; he also will hear their cry and will save them. The lord preserveth all them that love him, but all the wicked will he destroys. My mouth shall speak the praise of the lord and let all flesh bless his holy name for ever and ever."

FOR HEALTH

Yellow candle
Olive oil
Eucalyptus

Psalm 121

"I will lift up mine eyes unto the hills from whence cometh my help. My help cometh from the Lord which made heaven and earth. He will not suffer thy foot to be moved; he that keepeth thee will not slumber Behold, he that keepeth Israel shall neither slumber nor sleep. The Lord is thy keeper; the Lord is thy shade upon thy right hand. The sun shall not smite thee by day nor the moon by night. The Lord shall preserve thee from all evil; he shall preserve thy soul. The Lord shall preserve thy going out and thy coming in from this time forth and even for evermore."

COURAGE TO CONFRONT PROBLEMS

Red Santa Muerte candle
Olive oil
Allspice

Psalm 138 verse 7

" Though I walk in the midst of trouble, thou will revive me. Thou shalt stretch forth thine hand against the wrath of mine enemies and thy right hand shall save me."

COURAGE TO FACE ONE'S ENEMIES

Red Santa Muerte candle
Olive oil
Dragons Blood

Psalm 1

" Blessed is the man that walketh not in the counsel of the ungodly, nor standeth in the way of sinners, nor sitteth in the seat of the scornful. But his delight is in the law of the lord and in his law doth he meditate day and night. And he shall be planted like a tree by the rivers of water that bringeth forth his fruit in his season; his leaf also shall not wither and whatsoever he doeth shall prosper. The ungodly are not so, but are like the chaff which the wind driveth away. Therefore, the ungodly shall not stand in the congregation of the righteous. For the lord knoweth the way of the righteous but the way of the ungodly shall perish."

FINDING EMPLOYMENT

Red (or Green) Santa Muerte candle
Vetivert oil
Bistort

Psalm 24 verses 4-7

" He that hath clean hands and a pure heart, who hath not lifted up his soul unto vanity nor sworn deceitfully. He shall receive the blessing from the Lord and the righteousness from the God of his salvation. This the generation of them that seek him, that seek thy face, O Jacob. Selah. Lift up your heads, O ye gates and be ye lift up, ye everlasting doors and the king of glory shall come in."

GAIN CONFIDENCE

Red Santa Muerte candle
Olive oil
Frankincense

Psalm 70 verses 1-4

" Make haste, O God, to deliver me; make haste to help me, O lord. Let them be ashamed and confounded that seek after my soul: let them turn backward and put to confusion, that desire my hurt. Let them be turned back for a reward of their shame that say, Aha, Aha. Let all those that seek thee rejoice and be glad in thee and be glad in thee and let such as love thy salvation say continually, let God be magnified."

GUIDANCE/WISDOM

White Santa Muerte candle
Olive oil
Anise

Psalm 119 verses 25-32

" My soul cleaveth unto the dust: quicken thou me according to thy word. I have declared my ways and thou heardest me, teach me thy statues. Make me to understand the way of thy precepts, so shall I talk of thy wonderous works. My soul melteth for heaviness, strengthen thou me according to thy word. Remove from me the way of lying and grant me thy law graciously. I have chosen the way of truth, thy judgements have I laid before me. I have stuck unto thy testimonies. O lord, put me not to shame. I will run the way of thy commandments when thou shalt enlarge my heart."

PROTECT ONE'S HOME

White Santa Muerte candle
Olive oil
Cypress

Psalm 108 verses 1-5

"O God my heart is fixed-, I will sing and give praise even with my glory. Awake psaltery and harp, I myself will awake early. I will praise thee among the people. and I will sing praises unto thee among the nations. For thy mercy is great above the heavens and thy truth reacheth unto the clouds. Be thou exalted, O God, above the heavens and thy glory above the earth."

REUNITE LOVERS

Red Santa Muerte candle
Attraction oil
Violet flowers

Psalm 67
" God be merciful unto us and bless us and cause his face to shine upon us; Selah. That thy way may be known upon earth, thy saving health among all nations. Let the people praise thee, 0 God, let all the people praise thee. O let the nations be glad and sing for joy for thou shalt judge the people righteously and govern the nations upon earth. Selah. Let the people praise thee. Then shall the yield her increase and God, even our own God shall bless us. God shall bless us and all the ends of the earth shall fear him."

REVERSE EVIL BACK TO ONE'S ENEMIES

Black Santa Muerte candle
Reversible oil
Coriander

Psalm 82 verses 2-5

" How long will ye judge unjustly and accept the persons of the wicked? Selah. Defend the fatherless and the poor; do justice to the afflicted and needy. Deliver the poor and needy; rid them out of the hand of the wicked. They know not, neither will understand. They walk on in darkness; all the foundations of the earth are out of course."

SPIRITUAL GROWTH

White Santa Muerte candle
Olive oil
Lavender

Psalm 21 8-13

" Thine hand shall find out all thine enemies: thy right hand shall find out all those that hate thee. Thou shalt make them as a fiery oven in the time of thine anger. The lord shall swallow them up in his wrath and the fire shall devour them. Their fruit shall thou destroy from the earth and their seed from among the children of men. For they intended evil against thee; they imagined a mischievous device which they are not able to perform. Therefore shalt thou make them turn their back when thou shalt make ready thine arrows upon thy strings against the face of them. Be thou exalted, Lord, in thine own strength, so will we sing and praise thy power."

SUCCESS IN ONE'S ENDEAVORS

Red Santa Muerte
Olive oil
Primrose

Psalm 16 verses 7-11

" I will bless the Lord who hath given me counsel; my reins also instruct me in the night seasons. I have set the Lord always before me; because he is at my right hand, I shall not be moved. Therefore, my heart is glad and my glory rejoiceth; ·my flesh also shall rest in hope. For thou wilt not leave my soul in hell; neither wilt thou suffer thine Holy One to see corruption. Thou wilt show me thy presence is fullness of joy; at thy right hand there are pleasures for evermore."

WHEN JUSTICE HAS BEEN SERVED

Red Santa Muerte
Olive oil
Any pleasant-smelling incense

Psalm 124

"If it had not been the lord who was on our side, now may Israel say; if it had not been the lord who was on our side, when men rose up against us, then they had swallowed us up quick. When their wrath was kindled against us, then the waters had overwhelmed us. The stream had gone over our soul, then the proud waters had gone over our soul. Blessed be the lord, who hath not given us as prey to their teeth. Our soul is escaped as a bird out of the snare of the fowlers; the snare is broken and we are free. Our help is in the name of the lord, who made heaven and earth."

AMPARO AGAINST WITCHCRAFT

To make an amparo with Santa Muerte, get two Santa Muerte prayer cards and place them back to back. Seal up the sides and bottom with tape, glue, or by sewing them, thereby making a small packet. Then go in front of your Santa Muerte altar and pray the usual opening prayers.

Ask Santa Muerte to be your protection against hexes, curses, sorcery and witchcraft. Write your name on a small piece of brown paper and place this inside the prayer card packet. Then place some hair from your head and some nail clippings inside. Drop a few drops of Holy Water inside and blow some cigar smoke into the packet. Seal up the top of the packet, closing it off completely, and baptize it in the name of the Father, the Son, and the Holy Spirit using Holy Water. Then place it between your hands and pray over it.

Oh glorious Santa Muerte, Our Blessed Lady of Shadows, we beseech your presence and intervention. With your cloak, cover us with the mantle of your holy protection, and with your scythe, cut down all evil that presents itself in our lives, our homes, our jobs, and our paths. Through the great power, which God has given you, we ask that you banish all evil spirits, evil spells, witchcraft, hexes, curses, evil eyes, evil minds, and evil hearts from our presence. Our Most Holy Mother, look through the darkness that surrounds us, and remove all these evils. Amen.

Offer Santa Muerte some cigar smoke and a strong spirit, such as rum or tequila. Close with 1 Our Father. Keep this amparo under Santa Muerte's image or statue so he continues to protect you. Keep it hidden so no one else sees it. Every now and again bring it out and say the prayers again while holding it between your hands.

SANTA MUERTE NOVENA

Begin with the usual opening prayers (Our Father, 3 Hail Marys, Glory Be, St Michael, then the Invocational Prayer)
Prayer to be said each day before starting the novena:
Through the sign of the cross make the sign of the cross between your eyes ✠
From our enemies make the sign of the cross over your lips ✠
Free us, Oh Lord make the sign of the cross over your heart ✠
Through the intercession of the Santa Muerte. In the name of the Father ✠ the Son, and the Holy Spirit. Amen.

First Day
Santa Muerte, before your Divine Presence I kneel, begging a miracle from your hands, to alleviate my suffering. The Holy Trinity has formed you with Great Power; You who transverse all roads and pathways, who knows what men hold in their hearts, I beg of you, hear my prayer and answer me. (Mention your petition.)
(3 Our Fathers)

Second Day
Santa Muerte, beloved of my heart, do not abandon me without your protection. Oh, Holy and Immaculate Being of Light, I beg of thee to look with compassion upon me and my petition. (Mention your petition.) Oh, Holy Angel of God, who shall come to each and everyone one of us, who has the power to remove the soul from the flesh, I beg of thee to grant the petition I place before thee.
(Mention your petition.)
(3 Our Fathers)

Third Day
Santa Muerte, God has given you to us as a most powerful

intercessor in times of need. Have pity on me, though I am unworthy of it; and look with compassion upon my offering of tears, which I lay at the foot of your throne, confident in your protection and intercession. (Mention your petition.)

(3 Our Fathers)

Fourth Day

Santa Muerte, confident in your compassion for all beings, I come before you pleading for your intercession in my time of need. You who can travel the world in the blink of an eye, let my prayer be heard just as quickly, and on your swift wings, give me a sign of your assistance. (Mention petition.)

(3 Our Fathers)

Fifth Day

Santa Muerte, with open arms I welcome you into my life and home, assured that your Holy Presence will be a shadow of protection and grace upon me and those I love. Oh my saving angel, I beg of thee and thy power, grant this prayer I ask of you. (Mention your petition.)

(3 Our Fathers)

Sixth Day

Santa Muerte, with your cloak you cover your children with the shadow of your protection, and with your scythe you ward off all evil. Most gracious Mother! Behold me kneeling at your feet, pleading with you for this grace. (Mention your petition.)

(3 Our Fathers)

Seventh Day

Santa Muerte, you can alleviate my suffering, for the Divine Majesty has filled you with power. Confident in your compassion for your children, I come before you, and ask that my prayer be heard. (Mention your petition.)

(3 Our Fathers)

Eighth Day

Santa Muerte, your very name strikes fear in the heart of evil spirits, and even angels fall from their stations when

you spread your glorious wings.
With such power and majesty that you possess, I beg that you will use your Divine force to answer my prayers. (Mention your petition.)
(3 Our Fathers)

Ninth Day
Santa Muerte, I am confident that you will answer all prayers laid at your holy feet, and in thanks for the many blessings you will bestow upon me, I promise to love and honor you always. Stretch for your hand for me, and let my prayer be granted. (Mention your petition.)
(3 Our Fathers)

In the name of the Father ✠ , the Son , and the Holy Spirit. Amen.

MIRACULOUS MUERTE PRAYER

3 black candles
3 white candles
Say this prayer for 3 straight days at noon burning a white candle and at midnight with a black candle without fail and your prayer will be granted

Merciful mother of sorrows
Look down on us with pity
Your faithful that cry out to thee in this valley of tears
We pray that you hear our prayers and help us to obtain the comfort we need at this time
Merciful mother of sorrows
I pray that you hear my prayer on this day from heart
I seek your sole protection from the evil and harm that presses upon me,
I seek thy help so I do not fall before my enemy
Hold my hand and guide me on this path before me
I beg of thee to help me to grant this prayer with the blessings of Christ the grand redeemer
[say your need 3 times]..Never cease not once to pray my request on my behalf before the holy trinity
Helping me to gain victory over the snares and assaults from the devil
Grant to me thy courage, power and strength to be victorious over this test of my faith
Intercede for me further my gear mother of sorrows until the day I stand before St. Peter to be judged
I place my whole entire being in thy hands and pray I never fail before thee
I place all of my faith, hope love and trust upon thee to lift me up to the lord
Amen

TO REPAY SANTA MUERTE FOR HER FAVORS

When Santa Muerte answers your prayer, completes a work, or does something big for you, it is traditional to offer her a payment, or manda. One of the ways this can be done is a manda by candles. You take the statue that you worked with or the one who held the petition and place her on a safe, fireproof surface.

Place an incense burner next to her with a charoal for burning incense and have some white copal incense ready. Surround the statue and incense burner in a circle of twelve 6 inch taper candles, 4 white, 4 red, and 4 black, in an alternating sequence. Light the charcoal, place the copal on it, and light the candles.

Say the opening prayers, and give your thanks to Santa Muerte. Tell her how wonderful she is and that this manda is the payment for her work. Say the closing prayers and let the candles burn all the way down.

Once it's done, replace the statue on her altar, and put any left-over wax in a small brown paper bag, along with 7 dimes, and take it to the cemetery.

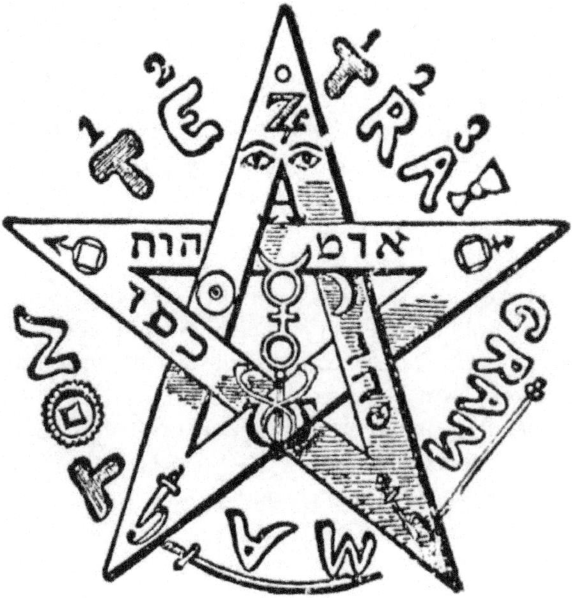
TETRAGRAMMATON

Printed in Great Britain
by Amazon